Money Folding
Making money into gifts you can spend

Jannie van Schuylenburg-Dekker

SEARCH PRESS

Introduction

Money is international and you can do so much with it! People often ask for money as a gift so that they can buy themselves something but it's so boring just to put it in an envelope. This book is full of great ideas on how to give money as a present. There is something for everyone: for him, for her, for the kids and for special occasions, and it's absolutely guaranteed that the receiver will love it. You will enjoy making the models and giving money as a gift.

With thanks to: Anja for the lovely assignment, Inge, Yvonne, Arja, for all their help, Marieke for all her inspiration during our coffee breaks and for the proofreading, Miranda and Paula for their meticulous adjustments to the drawings and text, Sushilla Kouwen for processing Gerhard's photos and for the use of her hands in those photos, and to Hans, who has always supported me.

First published in Great Britain 2008 by
Search Press Limited
Wellwood
North Farm Road
Tunbridge Wells
Kent TN2 3DR

ISBN 978-184448-329-7

Suppliers
Although every attempt has been made to ensure that all the materials and equipment used in this book are currently available, the Publishers cannot guarantee that this will always be the case. If you have difficulty in obtaining any of the items mentioned, then suitable alternatives should be used instead.
For details of suppliers, please visit the Search Press website: www.searchpress.com

Contents

For him
Shirt with pocket hand-kerchief 22

For her
Shirt 25

For her
Skirt 26
Fan card 26

For her
Gift envelope 28

For her
Hat 30

For her
Lotus 31

Kids corner
Money monster 34

Kids corner
Lanterns 35

Contents

Materials

- Bank notes
- Papicolor card
- CArt-us card
- Double-sided card
- Gold and silver card
- Origami paper, handmade paper, rainbow paper, fantasy paper, vellum, scrapbook paper
- Photo glue, Scotch Magic Tape (removable sticky tape), paper glue, 3D tape, double-sided sticky tape, stapler
- Gold braid, ribbon, elastic band and thin elastic, pins, cocktail sticks
- Florists' wire

- Card, Styrofoam, handkerchief
- Milk or fruit juice carton, empty and cleaned, old CD
- Mini cotter pins, mini brads
- Golden edge-stickers
- Stickles glitter glue
- Pinking shears
- Black felt tip pen
- Cutting mat
- Hobby knife
- Scissors
- Paper knife
- Pencil
- Ruler

Colour chart cArt-us-Papicolor/ Metric-Imperial Conversion

Comparing the two brands. Though not exactly the same, by using these colours you can create nice colour combinations.

cArt-us		Papicolor		Cm	Ins
white	0210	pearly white	30	1	3/8
natural	0211	carnation white	03	1.5	1/2
black	0219	raven black	01	2	3/4
cream	0241	cream	27	2.5	1
gold yellow	0247	buttercup yellow	10	3	1 1/4
spring green	0305	spring green	08	3.5	1 3/8
dark green	0309	Christman green	18	4	1 1/2
light blue	0391	azure blue	04	4.5	1 3/4
corn blue	0393	cornflower blue	05	5	2
violet	0425	violet	20	5.5	2 1/4
aqua	0427	dark blue	06	6	2 3/8
lilac	0453	lilac	14	6.5	2 3/4
soft pink	0480	salmon pink	25	7	2 3/4
warm pink	0485	cerise	33	7.5	3
dark red	0519	Christmas red	43	8	3 1/8
terracotta	0549	brick red	35	8.5	3 1/4
purple	0426	purple	46	9	3 1/2
ochre	0575	mustard yellow	48	9.5	3 1/2
green	0367	grass green	07	10	4
--		purple	13	15	6
met. Sapphire blue	0720	iris blue	31	20	7 7/8
--		turqoise	32	25	9 3/4
pearlised blue	0820	ice blue	42	30	11 7/8
--		lime green	50	35	13 3/4
cream	0241	peach	54		
centura gold	0904	gold	102		
pearl starfishwhite	0916	papiquilt white	111		

General technique

Can I use any kind of bank note?

This book contains models that are suitable for all sizes of bank notes. Sometimes the notes have to be folded smaller, or the model will become a little wider or higher; but this will not be a problem. If you want to know exactly what your bank note will look like when you have finished, practice first using a piece of paper cut to the same size.

Can you give me any tips about folding?

Try to fold as precisely as possible. Always keep your eye on the diagrams so that you know what the model should look like at each step. If you practice first with a piece of paper before making the actual model it will be easier.

Which side do I use?

If you look at the folding illustrations, you will see a light coloured side and a dark coloured side. The dark colour is the front of the bank note and the light colour is the back. Actually it is up to you which side you put on top. I generally use the following sides as the front.

What should I use to stick the notes together?

Always use photo glue or Scotch Magic Tape (removable tape), which won't damage the bank notes.

Where can I find more information about origami?

If you want to know more about folding, take a look at the following websites.
• OSN - Origami Sociëteit Nederland:
  www.origami-osn.nl
• BOS - British Origami Society:
  www.britishorigami.info
• Origami USA: www.origami-usa.org

Explanation of the folding symbols

Try to fold as precisely as possible. Always look at the next illustration so that you can see what it should look like when you have finished the fold.

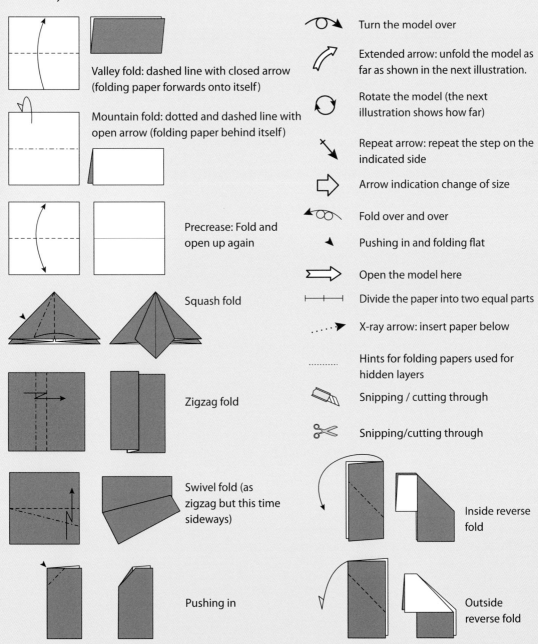

Valley fold: dashed line with closed arrow (folding paper forwards onto itself)

Mountain fold: dotted and dashed line with open arrow (folding paper behind itself)

Precrease: Fold and open up again

Squash fold

Zigzag fold

Swivel fold (as zigzag but this time sideways)

Pushing in

Turn the model over

Extended arrow: unfold the model as far as shown in the next illustration.

Rotate the model (the next illustration shows how far)

Repeat arrow: repeat the step on the indicated side

Arrow indication change of size

Fold over and over

Pushing in and folding flat

Open the model here

Divide the paper into two equal parts

X-ray arrow: insert paper below

Hints for folding papers used for hidden layers

Snipping / cutting through

Snipping/cutting through

Inside reverse fold

Outside reverse fold

Step by step

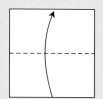

Valley fold: dashed line with closed arrow (folding paper forwards onto itself)

Fold the paper forwards, so that the white side is on the inside.

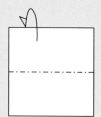

Mountain fold: dotted and dashed line with open arrow (folding paper behind itself)

Fold the paper behind, the white side will now be on the outside.

Squash fold

Start with double triangle (page 13).

Fold the crease and unfold.

Open the point and push it flat against the previously folded creases.

The point lies now flat.

Step by step

Pushing in

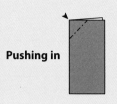

Fold and unfold.

Open the paper and push the point inwards.

Fold the paper back again on the existing creases.

Inside reverse fold
(Mountain fold with a valley fold arrow)

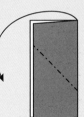

Fold and unfold.

Open the paper a little bit and push the paper inwards. Keep hold of the open side just under the crease.

Push the paper in as far as the creases.

Fold the paper flat once again using existing creases.

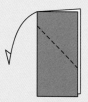

Outside reverse fold
(Valley fold with a mountain fold arrow)

Fold the crease and unfold.

Open the paper slightly. Gently hold the open side under the crease, holding one finger in between.

Pull the top section forwards.

Keep pulling forwards as far as the previously folded creases.

Fold the paper flat on these creases.

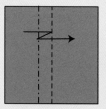

Zigzag fold

Make a mountain fold and a valley fold on the lines indicated. Take the mountain fold and slide it over the valley fold.

Flatten the model.

Step by step

Double square

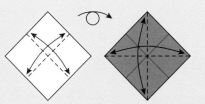 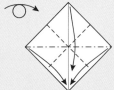  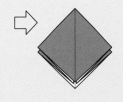

On the white side, fold the square side to side through the exact centre and unfold, so that you have a straight cross. Turn it over. Fold it twice corner to corner through the centre and unfold so that you have a diagonal cross. Turn the sheet over again.

Fold the points on the sides towards the bottom corner. The top corner will follow.

Fold the model flat. You should now have a double square.

Double triangle

 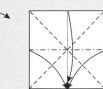

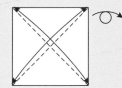

On the white side, fold the square twice corner to corner through the centre and unfold, so that it forms a diagonal cross. Turn it over. Fold it twice side to side through the centre and unfold so that you have a straight cross. Turn it over again.

Fold the midpoints of the sides to the midpoint of the bottom side. The upper side will be brought along.

Fold the model flat. You should now have a double triangle.

For him
Blue or white telephone

Design: Jannie van Schuylenburg

Everyone will love to have this cute telephone, so you can actually make them for the whole family.
(P) 20 violet or (P) 30 pearly white: A4 card, double-sided sticky tape.

Copy the model of the telephone onto the A4 card (see copy diagram) and extend the sides. Cut it out. Open the 'screen' with a knife or cut screen out and score along the dotted lines. Use double-sided sticky tape to secure the right hand side, below the screen, but leave the top side open. Fold a bank note to the right size and slide it behind the window, then fold the card in half.

For him
Blue or white telephone

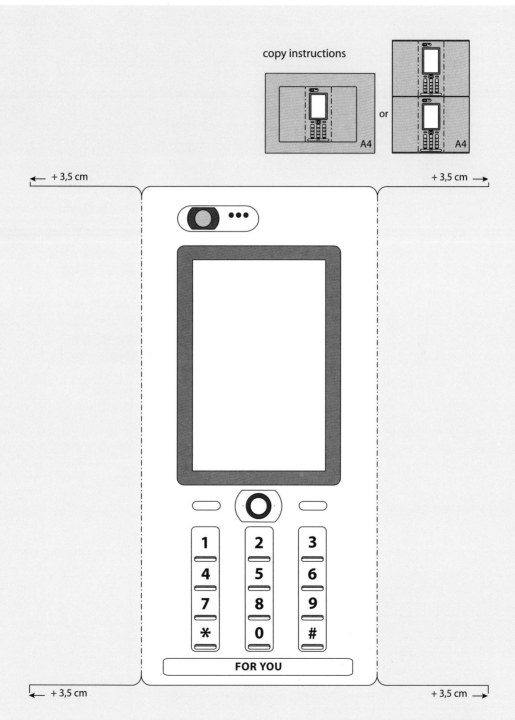

copy instructions

or

A4

A4

+ 3,5 cm

+ 3,5 cm

+ 3,5 cm

+ 3,5 cm

FOR YOU

For him
Car

Design: Jannie van Schuylenburg
Card idea: Tuzy Ibolyo

This is a great card for any car enthusiast.

Blue card: (P) 31 iris blue: double card 10.5 x 14.8 cm, (P) 03 carnation white: single card, 10 x 14.3 cm, (P) 43 Christmas red for the lights, (P) 01 black for the rear window, photo of a street.

Green card: (P) 07 grass green: double card 10.5 x 14.8 cm, (P) 03 carnation white: single card, 10 x 14.3 cm, (P) 43 Christmas red for the lights, (P) 01 black for the rear window, photo of a street.

Fold a bank note to make the car model. Stick the photo of the street onto the carnation white. Cut slits in the photo so that you can insert the edge of the roof and the sides of the car. Make the rear window and rear lights. Glue them with photo glue. Stick the card onto the double card. For the green card, do not fold in the corners of the boot (step 6).

01-EL-87

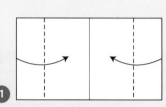

1 Fold the bank note in half and unfold. Fold the sides towards the middle to taste. Turn the model over.

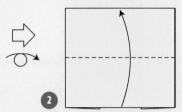

2 Fold the bottom edge towards the top.

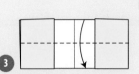

3 Fold the top layer towards the bottom.

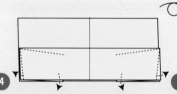

4 Pull the loose flaps downwards. The sides will now also move towards the outside slightly. Turn the model over.

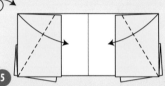

5 Fold the sides with an angle towards the middle.

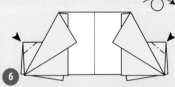

6 Precrease and push in the points. Turn the model over.

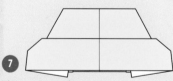

7 The car is ready.

8 Cut out the rear windscreen and glue it on. Make a number plate.

25-04-TA07

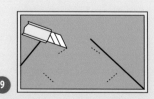

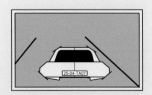

9 Take a photo or drawing of a street. Cut 4 slits and slide the corners of the roof and the sides of the car through the card.

For him
Shirt

Who says men aren't vain? They like to look good too!

(C) 210 white: double card 14.8 x 14.8 cm and a strip 3.5 x 11.8 cm, (C) 427 aqua blue: single card 14.7 x 14.7 cm and a strip 4 x 11.7 cm, 2 small blue buttons.

Prepare the white card as shown in model 2 of the shirt. Stick the aqua blue card behind the front sheet and place both strips in the centre. Fold the tie using a bank note and stick it onto the card. Draw part of a handkerchief on the front. Stick or sew the buttons onto the strip.

Model 1

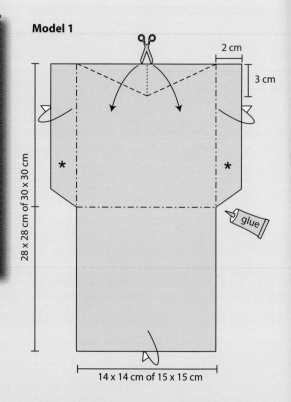

28 x 28 cm of 30 x 30 cm

2 cm

3 cm

glue

14 x 14 cm of 15 x 15 cm

Cutting diagram of the shirt as a bag for an inserted card. Make the card 3 mm smaller.

Model 2

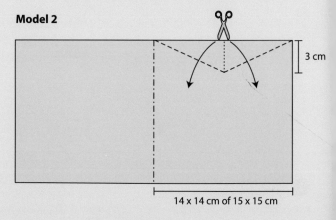

3 cm

14 x 14 cm of 15 x 15 cm

Cutting diagram for the shirt using a square card.

For him
Red shirt with bowtie

Design bowtie: Jannie van Schuylenburg

(P) 43 Christmas red: A4 sheet and strip measuring 3.5 x 11.8 cm,
(P) 03 carnation white: single card 14.7 x 14.7 cm and a strip
measuring 4 x 11.7 cm.

Make the red card following model 1 for the shirt. Stick both strips
in the centre. Fold a bank note into a tie and stick it onto the card.
Slide the carnation white card into the sleeve.

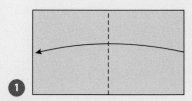

1

Fold the bank note in half.

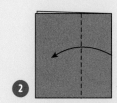

2

Fold the folded edge towards the left. Vary between half
and one third. The middle band will be wider the more
you fold over.

3

Fold the folded edge towards
the right against the edge.

4

Open the bank note
completely.

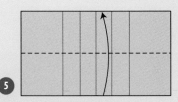

5

Valley fold the bank note
length-ways.

For him
Red shirt with bowtie

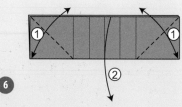

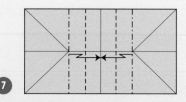

6 Fold the diagonal creases as shown and unfold. Unfold the bank note completely.

7 Using the existing lines, make a zigzag fold on each side. (See Step by step on page 12)

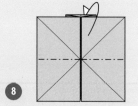

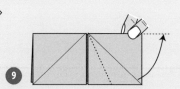

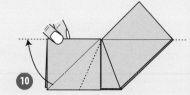

8 Fold the top side backwards.

9 Pull up the sides, so that the crease ending in the corner lies exactly horizontal.

10 Repeat on the other side.

For him
Red shirt with bowtie

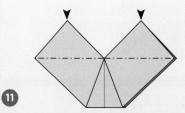

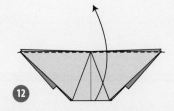

11

Push the top points towards the inside. They should go to the front of the inside layer. (See step by step page 11)

12

Unfold the front upwards.

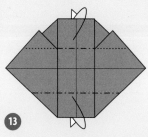

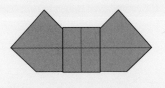

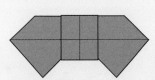

13

Fold the top section as far behind as you can. Fold the bottom section backwards as far as you wish.

14

The bow tie is finished and ready to use like this.

Or like this.

For him
Black/gold shirt with tie and pocket handkerchief

Design: Jannie van Schuylenburg

Double-sided card black/gold: A4 sheet, (P) 03 carnation white: single card 14.7 x 14.7 cm. Strip of fancy paper for the tie.

Prepare the double-sided card as shown in model 1 of the shirt, but don't glue it together just yet. Fold a bank note into a pocket handkerchief. Cut slits into the card and slide the pocket handkerchief into place. Fold the tie and stick it onto the card. Stick the card together and slide the carnation white card into the sleeve.

Tie

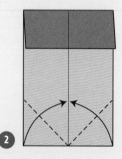

10 or 11 cm

① Fold the bank note in half and unfold. Fold down a strip.

② Fold the bottom corners to the central crease.

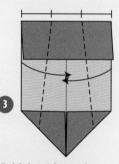

③ Fold the sides with an angle towards the central crease to taste. Turn it over.

④ The tie is finished.

Pocket handkerchief

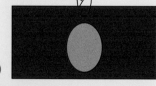

① Fold over a strip of the long side of the bank note.

② Fold the sides backwards and unfold. Fold them over so that the image is in the middle. This can vary depending on the bank note you are using. Turn over.

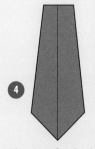

For him
Red/pink shirt with tie and pocket handkerchief

Double-sided card red/pink: double card 14.8 x 14.8 cm, (P) 30 pearly white: single card 14.7 x 14.7 cm.

Prepare the double-sided card as shown in model 2 of the shirt. Fold a bank note into a pocket handkerchief. As a variation you could fold the strip forwards. Cut slits into the card and slide the pocket handkerchief into place. Fold a bank note into a tie. Stick the tie in the centre. Stick the pearly white card behind the front sheet.

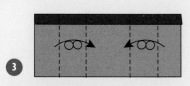

3 Fold the sides towards the creases, and then fold these as well.

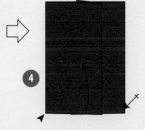

4 Push in the corner on the bottom side and fold the line above this upwards. Repeat on the other side.

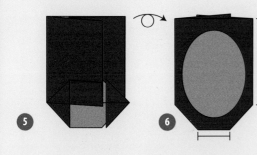

5 Turn the model over.

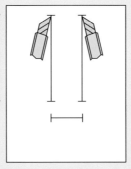

6 Draw the distance as illustrated on the example lines from step 6 onto the card and make 2 vertical cuts in the card. Slide the flaps on the back of the model through the slits.

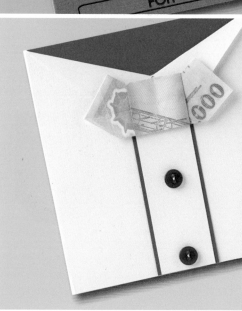

For her
Wardrobe - shirt

Design: Jannie van Schuylenburg

Plenty of room in this wardrobe! You can put away all your bits and pieces, then make yourself beautiful in the mirror.

(C) 575 ochre: A4 sheet, (C) 241 cream: A5 sheet. (C) 549 terracotta: 2 strips measuring 0.5 x 14.7 cm for the planks, gold card for the coat hangers, silver card, 2 pieces measuring 3.5 x 14 cm for the mirrors, origami paper 6 pieces measuring 2 x 4.75 for the boxes.

Fold both sides of the A4 ochre sheet 7.4 cm towards the centre. Stick the cream sheet in the middle of the card. Draw a curved line at the top (the curve should not be more than 3 cm) and cut out the cupboard along the curve. Stick the mirrors on the outside. Stick the strips for the shelves 5 cm from the top and 2 cm from the bottom. Stick the origami papers in the cupboard to form boxes. Draw the sides of the lids and write the contents on each. Cut a coat hanger out of gold card and stick it in the cupboard. Fold the bank notes into the shirt and the skirt and fix them 'in' the cupboard.

1

Fold the bank note in half and unfold. Divide the bank note into three, and unfold.

2

Fold down one of the long sides so that the ratio becomes 1:3. This will differ depending on the type of bank note you use.

3

On both sides fold the bank note in half and unfold. Turn it over.

4

Pick up the mountain fold and place the bottom point against the crease on the side (point of the arrow).

5

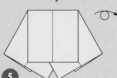

Turn the model over.

6

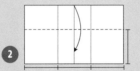

On the existing line, valley fold the bottom of the sleeve towards the top.

7

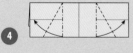

The model should now look like this. Turn over.

8

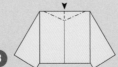

Push the top section towards the back and rear and make a mountain fold from the centre to the shoulders. You should now have an inverted triangle.

9

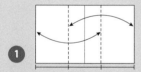

The shirt is finished.

For her
Wardrobe - skirt

Design: Jannie van Schuylenburg

Start with the coloured side at the top and fold
the first two steps of the fan (page 27).
Turn the model over.

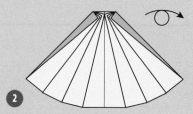

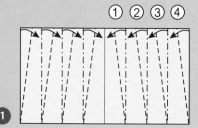

2

Turn the skirt over.

1

Take the first fold and put this at the top against the
centre line. At the bottom, the diagonal fold should
end on the vertical crease. Do this with the next strips,
and also on the opposite side but in mirror image.

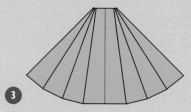

3

The skirt is finished.

For her
Fan card

Pink fan card
Fans are lovely to make, to give and to receive.

*(C) 480 soft pink: double card 14.8 x 14.8 cm, (C) 485 warm pink: single card 12.7 x 12.7 cm, (P) 03 carnation
white: 9,5 x 9,5 cm, hand made paper measuring 12 x 12 cm, 2 circles measuring 3 cm light and dark green,
gold cord, mini cotter pins.*

Stick the carnation white and the hand made paper onto the warm-pink card. Attach the mini cotter
pins to the corners, and then stick this onto the double soft-pink card. Fold a bank note into a fan. Let
the two circles overlap slightly and then fold them horizontally and vertically. Now you have a quarter
of a circle with a double edge. Make a small hole underneath and thread the cord through. Press it onto
the fan and stick it onto the cord.

For her
Fan card

Design: Jannie van Schuylenburg

Purple fan card

(C) 426 purple: double card, 10.5 x 14.8 cm plus a scrap of paper for underneath the fan, hand made paper measuring 9 x 13.5 cm, 2 circles measuring 3 cm pink and purple, gold braid, gold gel pen, pinking shears.

Stick the hand made paper onto the purple card. Fold a fan using a bank note. Secure it to the circles with braid in the same way as for the pink fan card. Cut the piece of the purple card so that it is slightly larger than the fan. Press the handle onto the fan, and stick onto the card.

Blue fan card

(P) 31 iris blue: double card, 10.5 x 14.8 cm, (P) 03 carnation white: 4.5 x 9 cm, gold paper, 7.5 x 12 cm, hand made paper measuring 7 x 11.5 cm, origami paper 5 x 5 cm, gold braid.

Stick the gold, hand made and carnation white papers onto the iris blue card. Draw a line on the blue and carnation white using a gold gel pen. For the fan, fold back ¼ of the bank note lengthways. It is now smaller. Carry on folding as usual but fold the last two sections behind. Fold the origami paper in half twice, and cut round with pinking shears. Thread a piece of braid through and press onto the fan. Stick the fan onto the card.

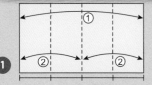

1 Fold the bank note in half and unfold. Fold the sides towards the centre and unfold.

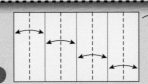

2 Make folds between the other folds. Turn the model over.

3 Take a fold and put this at the bottom against the edge of the next fold. At the top, the diagonal fold should end on the vertical crease.

4 Fold the front flap to the back as shown.

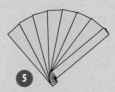

5 The fan is finished.

For her
Gift envelope

Design: Jannie van Schuylenburg

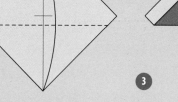

This is a lovely way to give money and you could also include a nice poem.
Double-sided origami paper, 15 x 15 cm.

Fold the envelope following the diagrams. Place the money inside.

1 Fold the small creases as shown.

2 Fold the top and bottom points to the top crease.

3 Fold the top to the bottom and unfold.

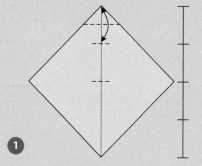

4 Fold the top layer over and over.

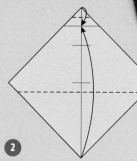

5 Fold the sides towards the top. The corner will now be on the line. (See arrow)

For her
Gift envelope

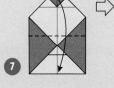

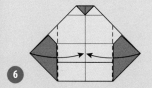

6 Fold the sides to the middle.

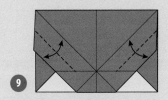

7 Fold the model in half.

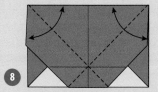

8 Precrease the front flap on both sides as shown.

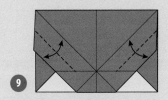

9 Make a crease between both creases just as far as is shown in the illustration.

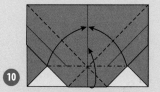

10 Make a double square, following the lines. (See step by step 'double square' on page 13)

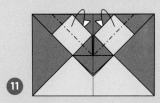

11 Make a mountain fold in the top layer.

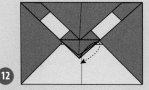

12 Insert the bottom of the flap into the envelope to fasten.

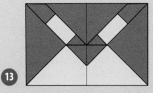

13 The money envelope is finished.

For her
Hat

Design: Jannie van Schuylenburg

How lovely to receive such a pretty hat, and it's fun to make too. Use her favourite colour.

Card Ø 17 cm, 2 small Styrofoam sheets, with a thickness of 2 or 2.5 cm Ø 10 cm, large handkerchief, elastic band, ribbon 35 cm long, small pins.

Make the hat from the Styrofoam following the instructions. Fold a bank note into a bow (page 19) and attach it to the hat.

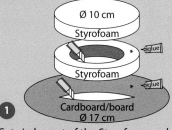

1 Cut circles out of the Styrofoam and the card as shown. Stick them on top of one another.

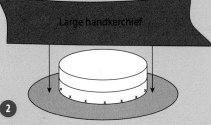

2 Place a large handkerchief over the top and pin it to the edge of the Styrofoam. (x) Stretch an elastic band across the top.

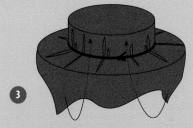

3 Spread the pleats out neatly and insert the points of the handkerchief in the opening at the bottom of the hat.

4 Pin a fancy ribbon to the hat and make a bow at the front.

For her
Lotus

Design: traditional

Perfect if she loves gardening.
Old CD, origami paper (if you want to replace some of the bank notes), elastic band.

Fold the bank notes into lotus flowers following the diagrams. If you don't want to use so many bank notes the diagrams calls for nine-you can replace some of the notes with coloured origami paper cut to size. For example, three matching papers for the inside petals, three bank notes for the outside petals and three green papers for the calyx leaves. You could use an elastic band instead of florists' wire to bind the flowers, etc, together. Place the lotus with the elastic band on the opening. Attach an unfolded paper clip lengthways under the elastic band at the back of the CD.

Start here with Origami paper

Start here with Bank note

1 Cut a square in half.

2 Fold it in half lengthways, and unfold.

3 Fold the corners to the centre line.

4 Fold the sides to the middle.

5 Fold this 9 x. For the lotus: 6 x bank notes for the flower (you could use a different colour for three of the inside petals) and 3 x green for the calyx. For the rose: 6 x red and 3 x green.

6 Place three modules on top of each other as shown.

Calyx + Outer petals + Inner petals

For her
Lotus on a CD

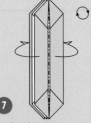

7

Make three seperate modules. Fold every module backwards and secure it temporary with a paperclip.

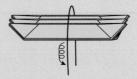

8

Place the three next to each other, remove the paperclips and secure them together with an elastic band. (Lotus on CD) Or use florists' wire for the flowers.

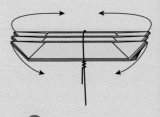

9

Fold the sides slightly towards each other.

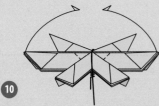

10

Pull the top layer towards the top. (See step by step: outside reverse fold page 12)

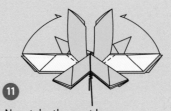

11

Now take the next layer.

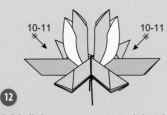

12

Fold all the 6 points as you did with the first two.

13

Press the calyx leaves flat and slightly towards the flower.

The lotus is finished.

When you are making the rose, pull the petals a little bit higher and the calyx leaves a little bit lower.

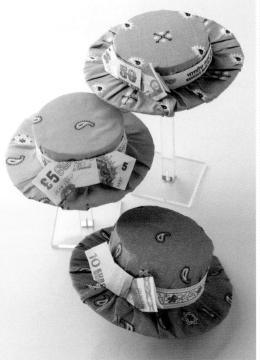

Kids corner
Money monster

Design: Jannie van Schuylenburg

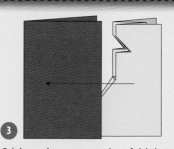

Watch out!!! They'll bite your finger....
Green: (P) 07 grass green: double outer card 10.5 x 14.8 cm
and (P) 08 spring green: double inner card 10 x 14.3 cm.
Pink: (P) 13 purple: double outer card 10.5 x 14.8 cm and
(P) 14 lilac: double inner card 10 x 14.3 cm.
Blue: (P) 06 dark blue: double outer card 10.5 x 14.8 cm and
(P) 42 ice blue: double inner card 10 x 14.3 cm.
(P) 01 black paper: 2 pieces 1.5 x 4 cm for the eyelashes and
2 x 8 cm for the moustache.

Basis for all models: Make the 'money monster' out of the inside card following the diagrams.
Affix the outside card using a matching colour.
Pink: Make the eyelashes following the pattern and stick them onto the eyelids.
Green: Make a moustache following the pattern and stick this just above the mouth
Fold a bank note in half twice, fold a small point and put it into the mouth.

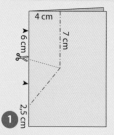

1

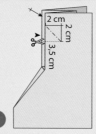

2

3

3D

1 Double card: 10 x 14.3 cm. Draw the cutting line and the fold line as shown. Cut the red line, score the fold line and push them both inwards.

2 Draw and cut the line as shown. Repeat on the other side. Push the eyelids inwards.

3 Stick on the outer card, unfold the card and look at the result.

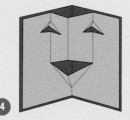

4

Eyelashes 2x

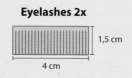

1,5 cm

4 cm

Moustache

1 cm

2 cm

8 cm

4 Make the eyelashes and/or a moustache following the cutting diagram. Place a bank note into the mouth.

Kids corner
Lanterns

Design: traditional

Lanterns on pink
Now we can have a great lantern procession…

(P) 14 lilac: double card, 10.5 x 21 cm, (P) 13 purple: single card, 8.5 x 19 cm, 3 origami paper, 7.5 x 7.5 cm, pinking shears.

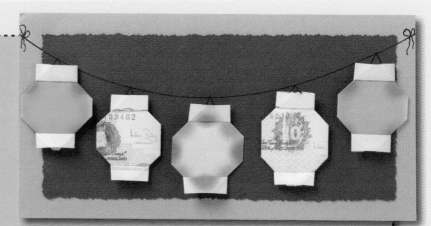

Fold the bank notes into lanterns. Using the origami paper, start at step 2. Using pinking shears cut along the edge of the purple card (first draw a guide line on the back). Stick this card onto the double card. Draw a black line and stick the lanterns along this line.

Lanterns on green with yellow

(P) 07 grass green: double card 10.5 x 21 cm, (P) 10 marigold yellow: single card 8.5 x 19 cm, 3 origami papers measuring 7.5 x 7.5 cm, pieces of gold braid, mini brads

Fold the bank notes and origami paper into lanterns as with the card above. Attach gold braid to the lanterns using Scotch tape. Using cotter pins, attach four lanterns to the yellow card. Stick this onto the green double card. Fix the remaining lantern to the centre of the green card with a mini brads. The lanterns should swing back and forth.

Kids corner
Lanterns

1 Fold the banknote in half.

2 Fold the sides to the middle.

3 Fold steps 2 to 5 of page 43 for the tall vase at the top and the bottom.

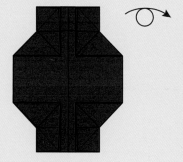

4 Turn the lantern over.

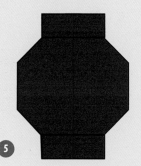

5 The lantern is finished.

Kids corner
Wallet

Design: unknown

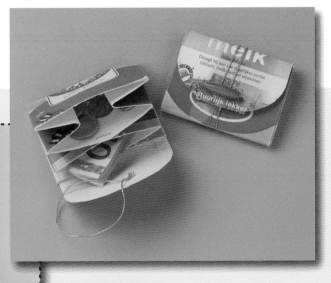

Anyone can make this wallet, and everyone will love receiving it. You can put other things in it as well as money.

Use an empty and thoroughly cleaned milk or fruit juice carton (or similar), thin (hat) elastic, button, small staples or strong double-sided sticky tape.

Fold the carton into an envelope, following the diagrams. Secure the centre with a small staple or strong double-sided sticky tape, and make a hole for the fastener. Thread the elastic band through the button and pull this through the hole. Put the money inside. Put the elastic band round the wallet and wind it around the button.

1

Cut the top and bottom sections out of a clean milk or juice carton.

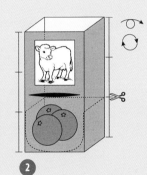

2

Divide into three parts and draw the flap on the bottom section. Cut away the rest of that section. Turn the wallet over.

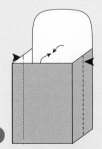

3

Push the sides inwards.

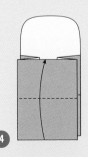

4

Fold the bottom section in two.

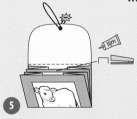

5

Staple or glue the sections together. Make a hole in the flap and attach an elastic band threaded with a bead or a button.

6

The wallet is finished.

Kids corner
Peacock

Design body: traditional

Peacock with fence

(C) 427 aqua blue: double card, 14.8 x 14.8 cm, rainbow paper: 14 x 14 cm, (C) 393 cornflower blue: 12.5 x 12.5 cm, (C) 575 ochre: 10 x 12.5 cm, (C) 549 terracotta: strips measuring 0.5 cm, origami paper 5.5 x 5.5 cm, 3D tape, white gel pen, black paper.

Cut a lengthways strip from the ochre card. Stick it onto the cornflower blue, rainbow and the double cards. Fold the origami paper to make the peacock's body and then fold the bank note to make the tail and attach them to the card. Use small strips of black paper for the feet. Make the fence by sticking the terracotta strips onto the card using 3D tape. Use a white gel pen to draw birds.

Peacock on rainbow paper

(C) 427 aqua blue: double card, 10.5 x 14.8 cm, rainbow paper: 10.5 x 15 cm, origami paper 5.5 x 5.5 cm, pinking shears, white gel pen, black paper.

Draw a line on the back of the rainbow paper and cut along this line with pinking shears. Stick this onto the double card. Draw a line using a white gel pen. Fold the origami paper to make the peacock's body and fold the bank note to make the tail, then attach these to the card. Use small strips of black for the feet.

Kids corner
Peacock

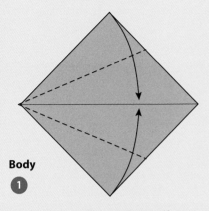

Body

1 Fold the square diagonally in half and unfold. Fold the sides to the crease, to make a kite.

2 Fold the kite in two.

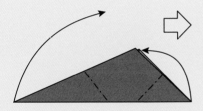

3 At the front and back, make an inside reverse fold as shown (See step by step page 11).

4 Make an inside reverse fold for the head.

5 The peacock's body is finished.

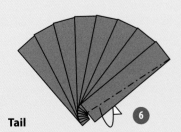

Tail

6 Use a bank note and fold as shown in steps 1 to 3 of the fan.

7 Fold the front flap with an angle as shown. Insert the tail into the back of the body.

Kids corner
Parasol

Stick the vellum or rough wallpaper (anaglypta) onto the pearly white card. Stick on the pieces of sand coloured paper to make the 'beach'. Stick the card onto the double card. Fold a bank note into a square and make the red origami paper 0.5 cm larger. Fold both of these into a parasol following the diagrams. Place the cocktail stick partly inside and attach to the card. Attach the sun and make a little sail boat using small pieces of white paper.

Parasol with a setting sun

Place the dark blue strip on top of the turquoise card. Stick on the pieces of sand-coloured paper to make the 'beach'. Stick the card onto the double card. Fold a bank note into a square and make the red origami paper 0.5 cm larger. Fold both of these into a parasol following the diagrams. Place the cocktail stick partly inside and attach to the card. Cut out part of the circle and stick on the sun. Decorate the beach with embellishments.

Kids corner
Parasol

Design: Jannie van Schuylenburg

1 Fold the bank note into a square.

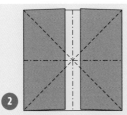

2 Make mountain folds and valley folds as shown.

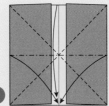

3 Fold the sides to the bottom centre. The top side will follow. (See step by step page 13 for the double triangle)

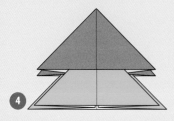

4 Take a square in a contrasting colour that is 0.5 cm larger than the bank note. Then fold a double triangle and insert it inside the bank note.

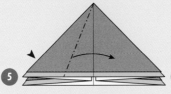

5 Precrease and squash fold, as shown. (See step by step page 10)

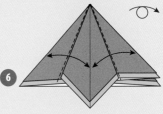

6 Precrease on both sides and turn the model over.

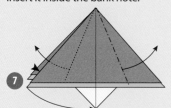

7 Press the left hand point flat at the centre point. The model will fall into shape because of the precreases.

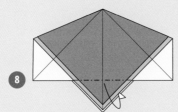

8 Fold the top two layers of the corner at the bottom towards the inside.

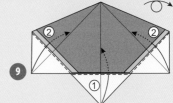

9 Fold the top layer of the bottom point towards the inside. Fold the top layer on both sides between the paper. Turn the model over.

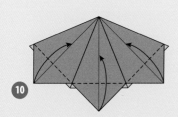

10 Fold all three points upwards.

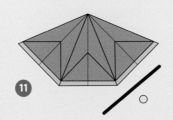

11 Glue a cocktail stick behind the parasol And a small coloured circle on top of this.

12 The parasol is finished.

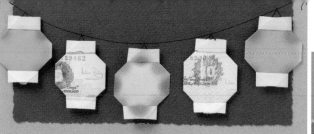

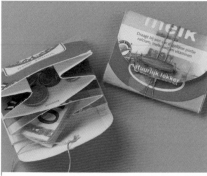

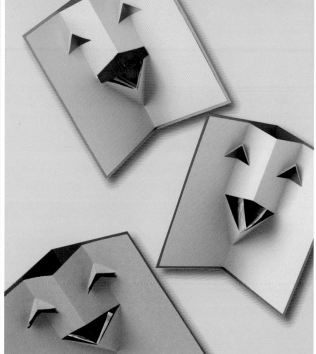

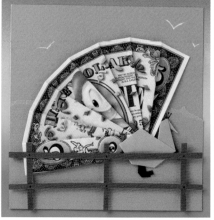

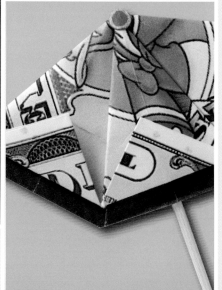

Congratulations
Vase

Design variations on lantern model: Jannie van Schuylenburg

Tall vase with flowers

(P) 20 violet: double card of 10.5 x 21 cm, (P) 30 pearly white: 9.5 x 20 cm and scraps for the flowers, (P) 31 iris blue: 9 x 19.5 cm, fantasy paper, black felt tip pen, Stickles glitter glue, 3D tape.

Stick the cards on top of one another. Fold one of the bank notes onto a vase and stick it onto the card. Cut the flowers out of white and fantasy paper and attach them using the 3D tape. Always put one white and one coloured flower together. Use a black felt tip pen to draw the stamens and decorate the heart with Stickles glitterglue.

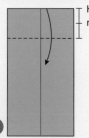

Height of the rim of the vase

1
Fold the bank note in half lengthways and unfold. Valley fold down a strip. The height of the rim of the vase should be half of the folded section.

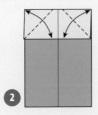

2
Fold the corners as shown and unfold.

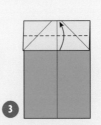

3
Fold the short section towards the top. Turn the model over.

4
Fold the triangles forwards using a valley fold on the existing creases.

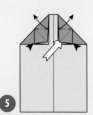

5
Open the layers. Push against the point and fold the edge towards the top.

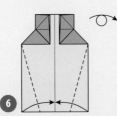

6
Fold the sides with an angle towards the middle. Turn the vase over.

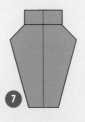

7
The tall vase is finished.

Large flower for the blue vase.

Vase with blossoms
Flowers are always perfect for that special occasion
(C) mother of pearl: double card 14.8 x 14.8 cm, (C) 309 dark green: 13 x 13 cm, (P) 50
shaded green: 12.5 x 12.5 cm, coloured origami paper, black felt tip pen, Stickles glitter glue.

Draw the branches for the blossoms on the coloured paper. Stick all the cards together. Cut out the blossoms from origami paper. Puff them out and attach along the branches using 3D tape. Cut out small leaves and stick them on. Sprinkle the Stickles glitter in the centre of the flowers. Fold a vase from the bank note and place it under the branch.

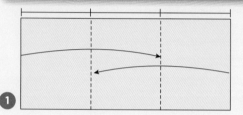

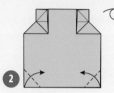

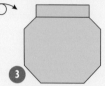

① Fold the bank note into three. Now continue with step 1 for the tall vase. Make a lower rim. Fold steps 1 to 5.

② Valley fold the bottom corners. Turn the vase over.

③ The round vase is finished.

Small blossoms for the round vase

Vase with yellow tulips
(C) 247 golden yellow: double card, 10.5 x 20 cm and scraps for the flowers, (C) 519 dark red:
9.7 x 19.2 cm, scraps of green for the stems, 3D tape.

Cut out 5 flowers from the yellow card and cut them into petals. Arrange the petals so that they form tulips. Stick the cards together and then attach the stems to the card. Use 3D tape to attach the flowers onto the stems. Fold a bank note into a vase, and attach this underneath the stems.

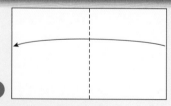

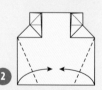

① Fold the bank note in half. Now continue with step 1 for the tall vase. Make the rim lower. Fold steps 1 to 5.

② Valley fold the corners diagonally.

③ Valley fold the bottom corners. Turn the vase over.

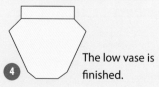

④ The low vase is finished.

Petals for the tulip: cut apart the petals.

Congratulations
Photo frames

Design: traditional

Fuchsia painting with gold
**You could hide a thoughtful text or message behind the painting.
What a lovely surprise**

*(P) 13 purple: double card, 10.5 x 10.5 cm, gold paper 4 pieces measuring
3 x 3 cm, gold sticker edging.*

Fold the 4 pieces of gold paper into a double triangle, following the diagrams for the photo frame. Fold the bank note so that the best image is on the top. Mark off the corners of the bank note on the front of the card. Attach the photo corners as shown on the model. Finish the card off with sticker edging.

Square photo frame

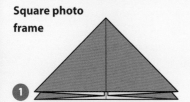

1 Make a total of four double triangles. (see step by step).

Round photo frame

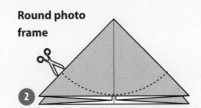

2 For a curved corner, cut the edge as shown.

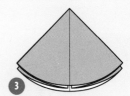

3 Make four of these.

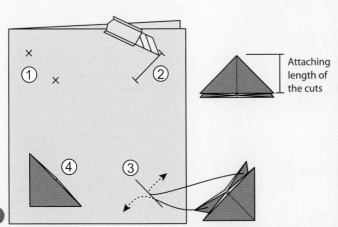

4

Attaching length of the cuts

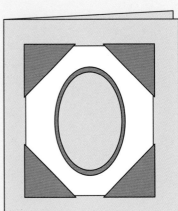

On the front of the card, use a pencil to mark the place where you want the corner point to be. Make four cuts the height of the corner. Slide the rear points of the corners through the slip. Fold a bank note to the correct size so that it fits into the photo frame.

Blue painting with Snow White

(P) 06 dark blue: double card 10.5 x 14.8 cm and one single card measuring 6.5 x 9.5 cm, fancy paper: 9 x 13 cm, yellow origami paper: 4 pieces 3 x 3 cm or 4 circles measuring 3 cm, white gel pen.

Fold the yellow papers following the diagrams for the photo frame. Fold a bank note so that the best image is on the top and mark off the corners on the single blue card. Attach the photo corners as shown on the model. Stick all the paper sheets together. Draw a picture and a nail with a white gel pen so that the painting 'hangs'.

Salmon coloured painting with lion

(P) 54 peach: double card measuring 10.5 x 14.8 cm, (P) 33 cerise: single card, 8.5 x 11.8 cm, 4 pieces of dark red origami paper measuring 3 x 3 cm, pinking shears, white gel pen.

Draw a square around the inside of the cerise card ½ cm in, and cut out with pinking shears. Fold the dark red papers following the diagrams for the photo frame. Fold a bank note so that the best image is on the top and mark off the points on the cerise card. Attach the photo corners as shown on the model. Stick the cards together. Draw lines and dots with a gel pen.

Bunch of roses

If a group of you want to give someone money as a gift, this is one way to do it.

Bank notes, origami paper to replace some of the bank notes if required, green origami paper for the leaves, red origami paper for the roses, florists' wire.

Fold the roses as shown in the diagrams. You can use matching origami paper in place of some of the bank notes if you want to. Make the red roses into a beautiful bouquet. If you are also giving a (dried flowers) bouquet as part of the gift you can use matching colours.

Congratulations
Heart on a ring

Design: Jannie van Schuylenburg

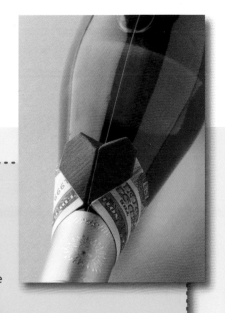

Everyone loves hearts and you can show how much you love someone.
Red origami paper, same size as the bank note.

Cut 2 strips the same size as the sides of the bank note or put the whole sheet inside. Fold the ring as shown here. Slide it onto a bottle or a candle.

1

Take a sheet of red paper the same size as the bank note and place it on top

2

Fold them together in half towards the bottom.

3

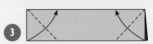

Fold the points of the first two layers towards the fold at the top.

4

Slide the left side backwards into the right, so that the folded lines meet each other.

5

Fold the 3 loose points backwards.

6

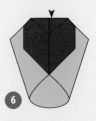

Push the top two layers down so that it forms an inverted triangle.

7

The heart is finished. Slide over the neck of a bottle or over a candle.

8

Variation: Fold the top point forwards in step 5.

47